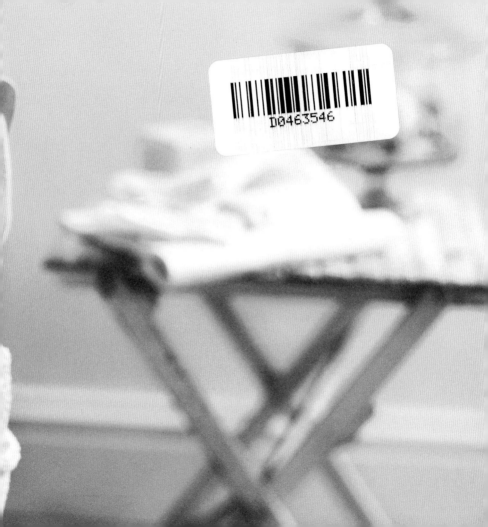

relax

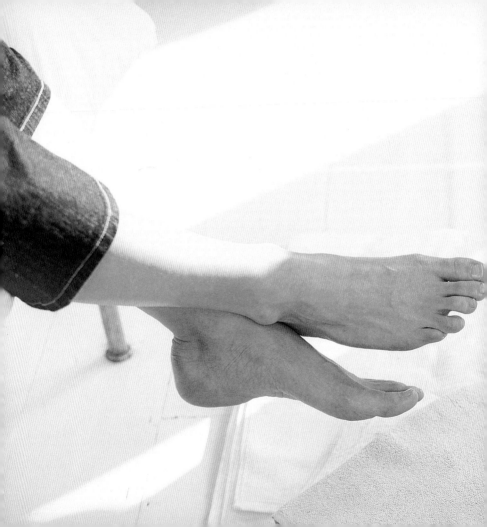

home spa

# relax

*Jo Glanville-Blackburn*

RYLAND
PETERS
& SMALL

LONDON NEW YORK

*To my three children Oliva, William, and Phoebe.*

**Designer** Sarah Walden
**Editor** Miriam Hyslop
**Picture Researcher** Emily Westlake
**Production** Tamsin Curwood
**Art Director** Gabriella Le Grazie
**Publishing Director** Alison Starling

First published in the United States in 2003
by Ryland Peters & Small, Inc.
519 Broadway, 5th Floor
New York NY10012
www.rylandpeters.com

Text, design, and photographs
© Ryland Peters & Small 2003
10 9 8 7 6 5 4

Printed and bound in China

ISBN 1 84172 381 9

If you are in any doubt about your health, please
consult your doctor before making any changes to
your usual dietary and wellbeing regime. Essential
oils are very powerful and potentially toxic if used
too liberally. Please follow the guidelines and never
use the oils neat on bare skin, unless advised
otherwise. This book is not suitable for anyone
during pregnancy.

# contents

# introduction

Whenever I need to unwind both mentally and physically,

I always end up in the bathroom; to the tub and the oils,

milks, salts, lotions, and potions that always manage to

make me feel like "me" again.

Creating a spa within the home allows you the time to treat all of the senses and to be more responsible about looking after your own body and its complete wellbeing. And it's easy to do. Simply make your bathroom a pampering

haven. Lower the lights; add the comforting aroma of frankincense, geranium, sandalwood, cedar, or cinnamon. Keep the room temperature warm and snug. Then choose the fluffiest towels, hang your bathrobe to warm on the radiator, play soulful music, and relax. This is your comfort zone.

Everything in this book is gentle, soothing, and relaxing for your mind, body, and spirit. So whenever you're feeling stressed, irritated, wound up, and need to relax … anytime … there's something here to help. Do as much as you want and need to, depending on how stressed you feel and how much time you have. All I ask is you try it all—again, and again.

unwind

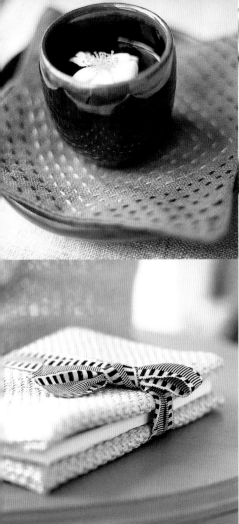

"If you can imagine it, you can achieve it. If you can dream it, you can become it."
*William Arthur Ward*

## calm down

Take it easy. The day's nearly done, so reap the positives from today and begin to unwind a tired stiff body ready for tomorrow with these relaxing body calmers:

Listen to some of your favorite classical music. It will help you relax.

Take a big stretch and extend all of those tense, tight muscles.

Try a little yoga. This yoga position is very relaxing, and is great for your spine: kneel on the floor, and stretch your arms right out in front of you until your forehead rests on the floor, too. Breathe slowly in and out. Hold for a count of ten.

Sit comfortably in a chair and lift your shoulders right up to your ears. Hold for a few seconds, then lower again. Repeat three or four times.

Add three to five drops of geranium essential oil to a bowl of hot water and leave it to diffuse into the air.

# relax your senses

Begin using your senses more to help you
relax and unwind.

**TOUCH** is an essential part of our well-being. Only think how comforting, uplifting, and reassuring a simple hug or an embrace can be. Touch is our first point of contact, both with others and ourselves. So include a little self-massage in your spa time, to your neck, shoulders, lower back, hands, and feet. Just add oil, then feel your way; you can't possibly do it wrong, and what feels good ultimately does you good.

**Five of the best relaxing oils to help you unwind:**

Balancing **LAVENDER** is the best leveler. It soothes mind and body when you're under pressure, and can treat a headache and insomnia.

Calming **CHAMOMILE** heals an irritable mind and irritable skin.

Restful **ROSE** works as a sensual sedative on overwrought emotions. It calms the nerves, lifts the spirits, and restores inner peace and tranquility.

Mood-enhancing **GERANIUM** acts as both a tonic and a sedative on the nerves, and is one of the best oils for relieving anxiety.

Soothing **SANDALWOOD** is both seductive and sedative. Burn the oil to scent the air and speed up relaxation.

**SMELL** Use aromatherapy to calm and balance your everyday feelings and emotions. There are many essential oils to choose from, but when it comes to finding the right oils for your needs at any given time, aromatherapists always say "trust your instincts." So in times of stress and anxiety, whichever aroma most appeals to you then, will benefit you the most. The easiest ways to use the oils are: add two or three drops to a tablespoon of sweet almond oil and rub into the temples and the back of your neck to help you unwind; or add four drops to a tissue or a room vaporizer and inhale deeply for a few minutes. In the bathroom, add six drops to your bath water or sprinkle them in the shower before stepping in or turning the water on.

# relax your mind

Practice switching off from stress on a regular basis, using meditation or visualization. Try one of these simple relaxation techniques:

**PRACTICE DEEP BREATHING** correctly. Close your eyes, place one hand on your abdomen (below the ribs) and the other on your chest. Breathe in slowly through your nose, and concentrate on moving only the lower hand.

When all is quiet—try a little **MEDITATION** to help clear your mind and focus on just one thing. It will help you sleep better, too. While seated, close your eyes, rest a hand on each leg, keep feet on the floor, and focus your breathing as above. Concentrate on relaxing your entire body, limb by limb, starting from your head. Imagine a warm light traveling down your back, flooding your limbs, down your legs, and out through your fingertips and your toes.

## relax your life

1 Light a relaxing, mood-enhancing candle to help you unwind. Choose one scented with frankincense, geranium, rosewood, myrrh, neroli, rose, or vetivert.

2 Find some peace. For five minutes each day, seek the sound of silence. Close your eyes, sit back, and listen.

3 Eat more slowly. Tension is often held in the jaw. Relax yourself and chew something slowly to help you unwind.

4 Drink a cup of chamomile tea. Sip it slowly to relax and settle the nerves.

5 Relax your breath.

6 Stroke your face ... eyes, temples, ears.

7 Scent the air around you. Light incense (in a well-ventilated room) rich in warm sensual notes of sandalwood, cedar, cinnamon, or vanilla.

8 Still finding it hard to switch off? Take five drops of lavender in a diffuser or oil burner to vaporize the oil. It will quickly calm you down.

9 Lie back, place a pillow under your knees to take the strain off your back, and breathe slowly and deeply for 10–15 minutes.

10 Play a game. Backgammon, chess, tiddlywinks ... bring out the child from within.

de-stress

"The bath is a haven
—a special place
where you can calmly
and quietly think,
reflect, or meditate."

*Horst Rechelbacher*

## bathing

When you need to relax, bathing is more
therapeutic than showering. When you're
immersed in water, nearly 90 percent of your
weight is displaced, so you feel lighter, slightly
suspended, and instantly at ease. Water is
the only medium that perfectly contours
and flows freely around your body, and warm
water promotes peace and tranquility by
lowering your blood pressure.

# blissful ways to bathe

Think of your bath as a haven of pure relaxation, rather than simply a way to get clean. Research has shown that our first response to "stress overload" is to retreat into the bathroom. So, a soothing soak must be one of the best ways to switch off at the end of a busy day. Set the scene: dim the lights, light a scented candle, and relax.

Rest your neck and shoulders in the bathtub with a **BATH PILLOW**. Lie back and imagine the waves gently lapping around your shoulders, and relax deeply. Practice **BREATHING DEEPLY**, close your eyes and imagine you are at the beach or by the pool—the most popular "happy" places to visualize. **SOAK** for a full 20 minutes. As you soak, put on a facemask, or place some soothing eye pads over your eyelids. For a soporific soak that will quickly relax a weary body: add three drops each of geranium, lavender, and neroli, or two drops each of frankincense, lavender, and sandalwood essential oils to a full bath, step in, and **IMMERSE YOURSELF** in the fragrant water. Make sure the water is slightly warmer than usual to relax your muscles.

# smoothing

Smoothing cream into
your skin is a sensual
pleasure that we rarely
devote enough time to.
The pleasure is as much
in the touch and caress
of ourselves—how rarely
do we do that—as in the
softness and aroma of
your favorite body cream.

Always follow bathing with a **BODY MOISTURIZER** to help seal moisture in the skin and prevent further dryness. Make it a ritual, and you will soon start to love and respect your body more.

Devote a little extra time to **DRY SKIN AREAS** on the soles of the feet, elbows, and knees. If you buff your skin (especially your feet), do so before soaking in the tub; otherwise, you may remove too much once it's softened.

Mix your own **SENSUAL BODY OIL**—three drops each of sandalwood and rose essential oils in two teaspoons of almond oil.

# body soothers

A worn and weary body seeks soothing sensations to help it unwind fully from top to toe.

Add three drops of lavender essential oil to a tablespoon of almond oil. **MASSAGE** onto temples, ear lobes, and the nape of the neck. Press firmly but gently in several places along the line from the neck to the shoulder. Hold for a count of 10 each time, then release.

Close your eyes, lay your palms over your eyes, and **GENTLY STROKE** your face slowly, downward. Using your four fingers on both eyebrows, press slowly, then release. Move the position of your fingers to the lower socket area (just under the eyes) and, again with light and slow pressure, repeat three times.

## skin soothers

Stressful times and situations often show through our skin, resulting in sudden inexplicable dry patches, rashes, and spots. So when skin feels in need of calm …

Make yourself a **CALMING** lavender face oil using two drops of lavender oil and one drop of valerian essential oil in a tablespoon of almond oil. Massage into stressed skin and around the nape of your neck before bed.

In emergencies (especially with spots), undiluted dab a little neat **LAVENDER OIL** directly onto your skin. It is a miraculous skin healer.

## diet

It is important to keep your blood sugar levels in balance to help you cope better with stress. That initial high you get from a sugar fix is soon followed by tiredness and irritability. Once your spirits plummet, you eat another cake—but your blood sugar level rises too quickly again—only to fall even more later. Instead:

Keep a supply of **HEALTHY SNACKS** on hand such as rice cakes, bananas, vegetable sticks (carrots, celery), Brazil nuts, or almonds.

**EAT FREQUENTLY**, and don't skip breakfast. Several well-balanced small meals eaten throughout the day keep blood sugar levels more stable. It can take up to four weeks to turn around a sweet tooth, but you will feel calmer and less stressed as a result.

If you have problems sleeping, **TRY EATING EARLIER** (try to allow two hours before going to bed) and remove all preservatives, additives, and stimulants from your diet—including alcohol and caffeine.

# balancing foods

1  No salad should be without avocado. Rich in vitamins A,
   B, C, and E, it is also high in potassium, which helps you
   to cope better with stress and anxiety.

2  Bananas are one of the best sources of potassium, zinc,
   and iron in one food, and are balancing and soothing to
   the digestive system.

3  Bump up your levels of vitamin B with brewer's yeast, and relieve
   stress and fatigue.

4  Papaya—with a squeeze of fresh lime—makes the perfect spa snack.
   It's a natural digestive (like lemon and pineapple)
   and cleanses the digestive system.

5  Dandelion coffee
   soothes the digestive
   system and helps
   associated sleep
   problems. Eat the
   iron-rich leaves
   in salads, too.

6 Garlic is a natural healer. An all-round tonic to a jaded system, it is commonly labeled antiviral, antibacterial, antifungal, and anticancer.

7 Kiwi fruit is great at relieving stress due to its high levels of potassium. It's also high in anti-aging vitamins C and E.

8 Celery is cleansing and anti-inflammatory, helping to soothe aching joints and relieve anxiety and depression.

9 Snack on sunflower seeds. High in protein and the B vitamins, they help to balance blood sugar levels, and so help with tiredness, stress, and irritability.

10 Oats calm the nerves, lower cholesterol, and balance blood sugar levels.

"Indulgence not only treats the body ... it treats the soul."

*Anne Semonin*

rituals

# rose heaven

Rose oil is euphoric, yet calming. It helps boost your confidence, makes you feel exquisite, and is perfect to use in times of stress or moments of self-doubt. Try this rose-scented body ritual.

Spritz a little **ROSEWATER** over your face and body, then add 10 drops of rose absolute to one ounce of almond oil, and six drops to a cupful of any lightly scented or unscented body cream that you have on hand. Diffuse a little rose oil in a room vaporizer. Now gently **SMOOTH** in the oil over your body, starting with your feet, working up your legs, hands to shoulders, chest, abdomen, back, and finishing on your face. Wrap yourself up warmly for 10 minutes to let the oil absorb, then apply the cream from your feet to your neck. Leave your face free from cream. **WRAP UP** again—under a comforter is nice (a perfect bedtime ritual)—and relax for 20 minutes.

# hands

Give yourself a paraffin wax hand treatment.
Favored by beauty salons and health spas,
this is the best way to soften and smooth dry
skin on hands or feet.

First **SOFTEN YOUR CUTICLES** by dipping your
fingertips in a small bowl of warm olive oil
for five minutes, and then massage in a
rich hand cream. Next coat your hands in
a layer of warm, melted paraffin wax
(available from most pharmacies), either
by dipping your hands in a small bowl or
painting it on with a brush. Let the wax
dry, then build up another four layers.
**WRAP A TOWEL** around your hands to keep
the heat in. Leave on for 15 minutes.
Take a nap or watch a relaxing romantic
movie. Then gently peel away the wax.
Your hands will never have felt so soft.

OLIVE OIL

## neck and shoulders

Try giving yourself a soothing back massage.

Place two tennis balls in a long sock, space them apart by two inches and tie a rubber band around the open end. **LIE DOWN** comfortably on the floor and position a ball on each side of your backbone. Now **GENTLY ROLL** yourself up and down, concentrating on any areas that are particularly tense or stiff.

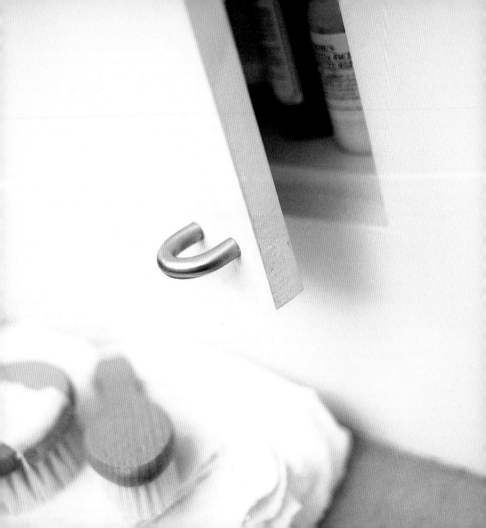

# hair treatment

**Treat your hair and scalp the way you do your body.**

Add two drops of **LAVENDER** and one drop of **CHAMOMILE** essential oil to two teaspoons of sweet almond oil. Great for stressed tresses or scalp problems, massage into the scalp, especially around the hairline. Wrap your hair up in a warm towel and relax for 20–30 minutes (make use of this time to try a new relaxation exercise or simply read a book). **SHAMPOO** once. Add the shampoo to your hair and scalp before adding any water. This way, your hair won't look oily afterward.

# relaxing facial

Smooth away the worries of the day ...

Thoroughly **CLEANSE** your face and neck to remove every trace of make-up and dirt.

**SOAK** a cotton ball with rosewater (or your own preferred toner) and sweep over your face to remove any excess cleanser.

Follow with a **DEEP-MOISTURIZING FACE MASK** to help smooth, soften, and pamper your skin. The best time to indulge is while you soak. The heat of the room allows the mask to penetrate your skin more effectively.

**MASSAGE** in a little rose face oil (four drops rose to two teaspoons sweet almond oil), paying particular attention to dry skin areas and tiny broken capillaries on the cheeks. Lie back and relax while it is absorbed into your skin.

# calm your eyes

**Try these instant relaxing eye tips:**

Soak two **CHAMOMILE TEA BAGS** in icy
water, lie back, and place on closed
eyelids for five minutes.

Have an **EYE MASK**. Add an extra thick layer of eye cream around your eyes and let it absorb. After ten minutes, wipe off any excess cream.

Give your eyes a **MASSAGE**. Sit with your elbows on a table in front of you. Interlock your fingers and place both thumbs on the inner corners of your brows. Let your head relax onto your thumbs. Hold for a count of five. Repeat along the brow.

# relaxing rituals

1 Spritz a little lavender water (six drops of
lavender oil in two ounces water) over your skin
and shoulders—anytime. Breathe in the mist.

2 Give yourself a manicure. Applying nail polish
forces you to sit quietly for at least 15 minutes.

3 Use petroleum jelly to remove mascara. It conditions
eyelashes and makes them look luscious.

4 Place a lavender bag under your pillow for a restful
night's sleep.

5 Soak aching feet in a hot foot bath with four drops of peppermint essential oil and a handful of Epsom salts.

6 Close your eyes, breathe calmly—and stroke a small smooth pebble between your fingers.

7 Shape your brows. It instantly makes your face look refreshed and more youthful.

8 Stroke fine facial lines and furrows. A relaxed, calm face is ultimately less lined.

9 Spritz a little of your favorite fragrance on your sheets before going to bed.

10 Whenever you feel overwhelmed, detach yourself from stress and escape to the sanctuary of a warm bath.

restore

"You are a product of your lifestyle—build in relaxation time and you will be better for it."

*Noella Gabriel*

## move to unwind

Sometimes when you're feeling stressed, it isn't enough just to sleep it off—you probably need to wind down. Yoga is the complete linking of the mind, body, and breath together. Simply sitting still, closing your eyes, and breathing—that is yoga. Do exercise that you enjoy. Not only does exercise improve circulation and strengthen your muscles; it helps you relax, too. If you need to unwind, go for a walk. Steal yourself 15 minutes to walk and think without purpose—that in itself is a luxury.

# posture

Slouching and poor posture create stress and tension throughout your body. Focus on improving the way you hold yourself and make attempts to better your posture.

Check your **POSTURE** by standing up straight and looking in a mirror. Does your neck jut forward (keep it straight), are your shoulders rounded (scrunch them up to your ears, then relax them down). Does your belly stick out? Pull it in.

Always be in **BALANCE**. Avoid carrying one heavy bag: carry two lighter bags instead. If you often carry a small child, alternate between hips.

## relaxing exercises

1 To calm down quickly, breathe in as slowly as you can (try to get to the count of ten), then breathe out equally slowly.

2 When you feel tense, rub the acupressure points that promote sleep: the center of the forehead and the back of the neck.

3 Add three to five drops of rose and/or sandalwood oil to a bowl of hot water and leave to diffuse into the air.

4 Clear your clutter. Space and order in your surroundings is more relaxing.

5 When stressed, massage this relaxing blend onto the pulse points: one drop each of chamomile, vetivert, and lavender oils in a tablespoon of oil.

6 Don't stand when you can sit, or sit when you can lie down. Put your feet up, lie quietly, and switch off.

7 Mix three drops each of chamomile, geranium and lavender essential oils in a two-ounce spray bottle of water, and use as a room freshener.

8 Breathe in deeply, as slowly as you can, then blow all the air out in one quick breath. Repeat several times.

9 Take 10 minutes to dream. Think creative thoughts, create goals, and help to realize them.

10 Create mental space. Take a few moments to reflect on your day, then put all your worries away in an imaginary box.

# sleep

Learn to use these relaxing and restful therapeutic
body rituals so you can create your own place of calm
to which you can return again and again and again.

"Trying to fit too much into the day is leaving us walking around in a chronic state of sleep deprivation," says Dr Gary Zammit, Director of The Sleep Disorders Institute at St. Luke's-Roosevelt Hospital in New York. Don't be a slave to rituals and routines. Learn how to take a break for you. Just 10 minutes every now and then makes a difference—and keeps you sane.

# useful addresses

## Complementary Therapies:

**Atlantic Institute of Aromatherapy**
16018 Saddlestring Drive
Tampa, FL 33612
t. 813 265 2222
www.atlanticinstitute.com

**Institute of Aromatherapy**
3108 Rt. 10 West
Denville, NJ 07834
t. 800 360 6468
www.instituteofaromatherapy
.com

**The American Center for the Alexander Technique, Inc.**
39 West 14th Street
Room 507
New York NY 10011
t. 212 633 2229
www.acatnyc.org

## Stockists and Suppliers:

**Aveda**
t. 866 823 1425 for stores
www.aveda.com

**Bath & Body Works**
t. 800 395 1001 for stores
www.bathandbodyworks.com

**Barneys New York**
660 Madison Avenue
New York NY 10019
t. 212 826 8900
www.barneys.com

**Bed Bath and Beyond**
410 East 61st Street
New York NY 10021
t. 800 462 3966 for stores
www.bedbathandbeyond.com

**Crabtree and Evelyn**
102 Peake Brook Road
Woodstock CT 06281-0167
www.crabtree-evelyn.com
for stores

**Crate & Barrel**
650 Madison Avenue
New York NY 10022
t. 800 967 6696 for stores
www.crateandbarrel.com

**Origins**
www.origins.com for stockists & stores.

**Sephora**
1500 Broadway #300
New York NY 10036
t. 877 737 4672 for stores
www.sephora.com

# credits

**Key: a=above, b=below, r=right, l=left, c=center**

*David Montgomery* 2-6, 7 a, 10-11, 13 ac, 14 inset, 15, 19, 21 al, 25 cr, 25 r, 26 inset, 27-31, 32 cl, 32 bl, 38, 39 b, 40, 41 main, 42 cl, 42 cr, 42 r, 43, 48-50, 54, 55 al, 62-63.

*Polly Wreford* 1, 13 bc, 13 b, 16, 20 r, 36 bl, 37 l, 39 al, 39 ar, 46, 55 cr, endpapers.

*Tom Leighton* 7 b, 17 r, 23 bc, 36 al, 51, 60-61, 64.

*Andrew Wood* 9 ar, 23 ar, 24, 42 l, 47 inset, 58-59.

*Jan Baldwin* 8 r, 20 l, 25 l, 25 cl, 52 l, 53 al.

*Dan Duchars* 8 l, 12, 13 a, 45.

*Chris Everard* 21 bl, 23 br, 39 ac, 44.

*Christopher Drake* 22, 23 bl, 55 bl.

*James Merrell* 41 inset, 56, 57 inset.

*Chris Tubbs* 52 r, 53 ar, 53 br.

*Debi Treloar* 26 main, 55 br, 57 main.

*Alan Williams* 21 ar, 32-33 main, 55 ar.

*Francesca Yorke* 14 main, 18, 32 al.

*David Brittain* 37 r, 55 bc.

*William Lingwood* 34-35.

*David Loftus* 9 al, 36 br.

*Caroline Arber* 9 bl.

*Ray Main* 17 l.

*Pia Tryde* 23 al.

The publisher would like to thank all the homeowners and designers who allowed us to photograph their homes and work.

# acknowledgments

The author would like to thank the following for all their help in the making of *Home Spa: Relax* and *Vitality*: Fiona Lindsay of Limelight Management and Alison Starling of Ryland Peters & Small for making it happen; my husband James Stanton for always running the bath; Noella Gabriel, aromatherapist and Director of Product and Treatment Development for Elemis, for her wisdom; Glenda Taylor, aromatherapist, for her encouragement; nutritionist Ann-Louise Gittleman for her endless advice; Reiki healer Mark Hegarty for his focus.

page 24–5 Research by Origins, Estee Lauder Worldwide.